ACTING 101

The How-to guide for beginning Actors

by

Daniel Whitehurst

Table of Contents

INTRODUCTION

Hollywood isn't the only place where a person can break into acting, you can do so just about anywhere you find commercial market. I wrote this for people who want to break into acting, but don't know how. It is a step by step instructional guide to help you get started in screen acting. Everything here is based on true life experience on what to do and what not to do.

Acting 101, The how-to guide for beginning actors is a book designed to cut to the chase because I designed it that way. We can talk about technique and method acting until the cows come home but let's face it, what you really want to know is how to get in, and that's what this book is about; the business side of acting.

I am not knocking technique, or training, those things are important, but there are classes for that. Most classes rarely teach you about head shots, set etiquette, resumes, and that's what makes my book so different, it tells you what you need to know to get started in film and television acting.

This book is made up in two parts; knowledge and reference. The knowledge part will tell you everything you need to know about getting started and the reference has a listing of photographers, talent agencies and unions in New York, Los Angeles, and everywhere in between.

With this book I will show you what my high school drama teachers and college professors could not teach me; how to get started.

I'll teach you about talent agents, casting companies, contracts, unions, auditions, and type casting and training. We will also learn the difference between commercial acting and television and film acting.

This book will not make you rich and famous but what it will do is provide you with some knowledge that will help you make informed decisions about your career and give you the potential to getting one step closer to your goal.

CHAPTER ONE

GETTING STARTED

There are probably thousands of actors in the United States, if not more, but what differentiates the professionals from those doing it as a hobby is knowledge; not just knowledge of your craft, but knowledge of how the industry works. Knowing who to talk to, and who not to talk to, and having the right tools, so without further ado lets get started.

STEP ONE: GET YOUR HEAD SHOT

Business people leave business cards, actors leave headshots. The purpose of a headshot is to have a professional package to present to legitimate agencies and casting directors. If want to attract legitimate agencies, then you must use legitimate marketing tools.

The casting director wants to see what you look like from the shoulders up, so get ready for your close up.

For this you will need to contact a professional, someone who specializes in entertainment headshots. Check your yellow pages or go on line to shop and compare. Prices vary from one place to another. In Florida it's not unheard of to pay $250 or more for a photo shoot, in Chicago its not unheard of to pay $600 or more it's all depends on where you live.

Professional headshots can be a bit pricey, but this is an investment in your career. Sometimes, it takes money to make money. Generally this is a business transaction, and whenever you invest money into a business you stand not only a good chance of making your money back, but writing it off in your taxes. (See your tax professional)

By the time your session is over, you will have many proofs to choose from, and you'll have a chance to choose the head shot that best represents you. If you're trying to get print work, then you can build your portfolio, or composite. Also the internet is beginning to play a vital role in casting, a CD with your photos will come in handy when asked to send your headshot over the internet..

STEP TWO: MAKE YOUR COVER LETTER AND RE-SUME

Like most jobs, you need a resume, only the format you use as an actor is different from a resume in any other industry. The resume has two parts: the top portion consists of your stats; name, height, weight, contact information, and generally the agency's name, telephone and fax number. The second part consist of where you worked it the past starting with film, and finally ending with special skills.

If you're just starting out, you may not have all these things to put on your resume so in the mean time seek experience such as your school or community play, or audition student films at the college near you.

Now if you want quick and easy use a stapler or glue, but if you want a clean professional look, simply take them over to FedexKinko's, Staples or wherever office products and services are sold. Tell them you want your resume copied to the back of your headshots. Copy about thirty headshots to start with. Note to you; some of your photos will be ruined and it may take a day or two to get them back but your photos and resume will be of good quality, and it will look professional. Once you have your head shots and resume in hand you are ready for distribution to various agencies and casting directors.

When petitioning talent agencies it is best to begin with a cover letter in business format briefly telling them who you are and that you are seeking representation leaving a contact number and your email address.

With the cover letter, send one head shot with your resume on the back. On that resume place your name at the top center of the page. Next place your stats on the left side such as eye color, hair color, height and weight, and never put your age or date of birth, unless you're a minor. The right side is usually for contact information which you would leave blank because there you would place the agencies stamp, besides that your contact information is in the cover letter and that is something only your agent should have.

Next you begin to list your credits starting in the order that they apply; Film, Television, Commercials, Industrials, Print, Stage, Training, and Special Training.

Film has three categories; Feature, Independent, and Student film in that order. Television would be any sitcom which usually relates to comedy or series which generally relates to drama.

You then list commercials such as a television ad, and then industrials which are the training films employees use to train. Print would be the work you do for billboards and catalogues and followed by your training acting for camera classes or even stunt school. Last would be your special skills, maybe you're a nurse or a teacher, maybe you can ride a horse or you've done rodeo.

On your resume you will list the roles you've played and the name of the production company. Here is an example of an actor's resume..... okay it's mine. Included is a sample of a cover letter as well as a resume worksheet.

Agency's name

Agency's address

Dear Lead Agent,

(It's always a good idea to find out who this is)

I'm currently seeking representation and have heard very positive things about your agency. I have not only had training but I have experience on screen as well as stage as indicted by my resume and headshot. I look forward to hearing from you.

Thank you,

Daniel Whitehurst

(407) 341-XXXX

daniellwhitehurst@myemailaddress.com

Daniel Whitehurst

Eyes: Brown
Hair: Black
Height: 5'7.5"
Weight: 235 lb.

Film

Final Destination 4	Extra	Avery Pix Inc.
Willie	Hotel Guest	Avanti Productions

Television

Sheena	Extra	Corsica Productions
Taina (Episode 105)	Background	Uptown Productions

Commercials

ESPN	Extra	Backyard Productions
Disney's Princess on Ice	Extra (Dad)	Go Films

Stage

A Raisin in the Sun	Assagi	Walker

Industrial

AWANA	Extra (Greg)	The Crawford Group
Universal Studios Vacations	Tourist	Universal Production

Training

Actors-on Camera Training	Shauna Bartel	Orlando, Fl
Commercial Training	Shauna Bartel	Orlando, Fl

Puppetry Arts: Skilled in hand, and body puppets.

Resume Worksheet

Name_____

Hair color   _____   Contact number

Eye color_____Fax number (If Applicable)

Weight_____height_____

Film   Role   Production Company

_____

_____

Television   Role   Production Company

_____

_____

Commercial   Role   Production Company

_____

_____

Stage   Role   Production Company

_____

_____

Training:

Special Skills:

STEP THREE: FIND AN AGENT

A talent agent is someone who finds you work, and negotiate a fair rate of pay. It is in their best interest as well as yours to do so. A talent agency never ask for money up front, because they are paid by casting directors to find talent and take anywhere between 10 to 20% commission from you when you get paid.

Finding an agent can be costly if you don't know what you're doing, many people who try to pass themselves off as agents are not agents, and are looking to rip you off, so before I tell you what to look for, I'm going to tell you what to avoid;

* Anyone who ask for huge amounts of money up front

* Anyone who wants to set you up with his or her photographer. (They're getting a kick back)

* Anyone who wants to put you through school or classes.

* Anyone who tries to pressure by making you believe it's a once in a life time deal and if you don't do it now "You'll never get another opportunity like this again."

* Anyone who advertise through news paper want ads or radio.

I've seen agencies at work; they don't have time to train you and put you through class. An agent does not have time to hold your hand, set you up with a photographer, and they never ask for money up front. They get their money when you get your money. An agent is constantly on the phone with clients, they don't have time for long conversation. When you go to an agency your in and out. It's fast pace, get it done, come with your game face or go home, kind of business. I'm not going to say who you should or should not go to, but in the back of the book will be a list of photographers, agencies, unions, associations, and schools.

I was lucky, I moved next door to someone who was in the business and told me everything I needed to get started. Understand that instead of going to a professional photographer, I went to Glamour Shots ® after that I asked them to sign a copyright release form and took my photos down to Photo Scan® and had duplicates printed. After that I attempted to make out a resume and at the time the only thing I had was a stage credit of Assagi in Raisin in the Sun. I then took my resume and stabled it to the back of my head shot and took a ride down to Central Florida Talent and registered. Next they had me sign a non-exclusive contract, and advised me to seek other agents so that I could get more work. They also advised me not to sign any exclusive contracts because I'd be stuck with someone who may or may not be able to find me work. With Azuree Talent there was no contract, if I remember correctly I mailed them the head shots unsolicited, which I don't believe you should do, because I got a phone call with a concerned voice on the other end, who basically said to me, call us when you have more experience. Although they called me the same day for the television show Sheena, so you never know. There is more than one way to skin a cat this is just how I skinned mine.

Now that I've made all of the stupid mistakes let me tell you what I should have done;

* I should have taken my head shots at a professional entertainment photographer.

* Prepare a resume, and have the duplicates made and place the resume on the back via FedexKinkos®

* Send letters and one head shot and resume requesting representation and have a monologue ready in case I was called in for a reading.

* Wait for a phone call.

The agent will initially call you for extra work, but in order to qualify for principal you may be required to read a monologue, which is necessary for speaking roles. Walk ons pay $75 to $100 per day, speaking roles pay at a higher rate which usually ranges from $400 per day you are non-union.

It is up to you whether or not you want to take the job, but if you decided to take the job, you must be reliable. Show up for your casting call on time, do what is asked of you while on the set, and pay the agency their percentage on time.

If you are not sure that you can show up, don't accept the job, politely decline and the agent will understand. It's better to be honest up front. Hollywood is very small so if you tick off the wrong people, it could be detrimental to your career.

As I said, their job is to find work for their clients and negotiate pay rate, meals and breaks. Here's how it works; someone or some company comes up with an idea for a commercial, film, television show, or maybe a print ad, never the less, they hire a production company, the production company hires a casting director, the casting director pays a fee to the talent agent to look at their data base of talent maybe a binder with headshots or composites.

The casting director tells the talent agent who he would like to see and the talent agent calls the talent to see if they're available for an audition or available to be cast as an extra, and the talent or parent says yes or no based on their availability.

That being said, no talent agent that I know have the time to teach classes, take pictures, set you up with a photographer, set up your portfolio, or introduce you to any top producer of any show, nor do they have time to tell you their life story and charge you ridiculous fees for coming to their office a talent agent represents you should be free of charge. The only thing you should pay an agent is the 20% commission which is paid with the money you receive from the production. The checks I've received already has the 20% deducted leaving me with the remanding balance.

As I've said before the talent agent or agency represents professional talent, it cost nothing to be represented. Yes I'm repeating myself but thats because I don't want to see you get ripped off.

EXTRA CASTING COMPANY

Principal actors are cast through agents, and so are *extras* which are entry level how ever if you don't think you're ready for all of the above then an Extra Casting Company may be for you. If you're just getting started you are most likely to land an extra role before landing a principal role which goes with out saying. Extras are the people in the background, they are the people at the cocktail party, they're the people walking the street, or the kids in the classroom.

Like any job there is a hierarchy. In this case the principal actors are at the top of the food chain. As an extra you will be at the bottom, but that doesn't mean your not important. Extras adds realism to the production and its not unheard of for an extra to be bumped up to a one liner because someone didn't show up, especially if you extra regularly on a television production, you're able to start networking and building relationships.

Background Entertainment is a company well known and well respected in Orlando, FL. They have employed hundreds perhaps thousands of people in commercials and films that have come to Central Florida. An extra company is often confused with an agency, but it's not the same, although many agencies start out as extra company.

Extras are paid $75 to $250 for a day of work which can usually last from 4 hours to 12 hours. Paychecks are delivered through the mail. Feature films pay about every 2-3 weeks and commercials and print pay every 30-45 days. Understand this, an extra company is not an agent but the wonderful thing about being an extra is that it gives you a chance to build your resume while you build a career.

Here is how it works; There is generally a casting call for extras, calling for all types of people. When you arrive at the location, you will register and they will ask for your name address, and stats such as shoe size, dress size, eye color, hair color etc. and your email address. They may ask for a small fee of maybe $20 to take your picture and place you in their data base. Once you are in they may have a mass orientation telling you basically that if you commit to a job you must be on time, then you go home and wait.

While you're waiting, a film company will hire the casting company to find actors for an up coming film. They pay a fee to the extra casting company and let them know what they're looking for. The extra casting company may send out an email to everyone on the list who meet the specifications or they may send out a mass email asking whether or not you're available.

You will also be given information like the rate that they will be paying you, and possibly the scenario, as well as point of contacts. Once you submit your name and they book you, you're committed. If for some reason you are not able to keep your appointment, call someone at the extra casting company and let them know immediately.

CASTING OVER THE INTERNET

Some agencies have a website, and have placed their company and company logo on myspace and facebook. Many actors have build web pages, blogs, and twitter, as well as facebook and myspace for networking with other actors, casting directors, agencies, and connecting with fans.

The flip side of that is there are many internet casting companies popping up, and for a monthly fee will connect you with productions and auditions in Hollywood or your local area.

The only thing I can say about the internet casting is, I only deal with people and companies I know.

ESTABLISHING A REPUTATION

No one in their right mind wants to work with difficult people, and neither do agents, cast nor crew. There are several ways to establish a reputation; the way you represent yourself in your head shot and resume, the way you handle rejection, talk to people over the phone, and especially the way you deal with people in person, whether or not you arrive on time, your professionalism on set, or lack there of, and now a days, the way you present yourself online. People talk and if you throw a tantrum in an audition or on set they'll be talking about it five years from now.

CHAPTER TWO
SET ETIQUETTE

The purpose of this chapter is to teach you Set Etiquette or how not to get yourself fired, and prolong your career. If I may quote Jamie Fox the first lesson in acting is to "Act like you got some sense."

WHAT'S EXPECTED OF YOU

First things first, you're expected to show up on time, but that goes with out saying, you're expected to bring wardrobe and follow the guidelines you received in the email.

A 5:00am call time is not unheard of, you should have received the address in the email and used map quest to find the location before getting on the road. If you get lost its good to call ahead.

When you arrive sign in with the casting director, and report to wardrobe. If you are principal you will be shown to your trailer if you're filming outside or your dressing room if you're filming inside, if you're an extra you will be shown to the tent if outside, or a green room if inside.

Either way, your job is simple, if you're an extra; do what you're told when you're told to do it, and how you're told to do it. Don't get creative, that's the director's job. There are a lot of dos and don't s so make sure you follow them. If you're principal deliver the lines as the director expects you to.

*Don't take pictures of the set or cast, this is the fastest way to lose your job.

* Don't approach principal actors and start asking for auto-graphs, be the professional you say you are and do the job that you're paid to do.

* If you're not sure ask. If you need stage direction, or are un-sure of your blocking, what ever time is money, and you'll save lots of both if you get it right the first time.

* Don't discuss your salary or compare agencies with other ac-tors. It's very unprofessional, and it can get you into a lot of trouble. If you're just starting out you're going to get the en-try rate. Those that have been around longer may be able to negotiate more. Some get paid more than others, not just in this business but in any job you do, and discussing salaries out in the open can put your agent and others in an awkward and uncomfortable position, as well as shorten your career.

* Most important, if the director corrects you for doing some-thing wrong during the take, for heavens sake don't waste time making excuses, just say okay and make the correction, time is money.

* When you are on set always try to quietly figure out who is in charge of giving directions.

* Once you've figured out who's in charge, usually an assistant director or AD, pay close attention and watch for their direc-tion. Just remember that on the set time is money, and if you are not paying attention when they call you, it can delay the project.

* Don't say negative things about anyone, especially your
agent. It can and will get back to them, and you don't want
that to happen. If you're not happy with your agent I'm sure
there are others to choose from.

WHAT TO EXPECT

I don't know if you've ever heard the term "Hurry up and wait"
but until the director calls for you, pretty much that is what
you do. The production is made up of cast and crew; the cast
are the actors and the crew is everyone from the director to the
gaffer. You may get a call time around 5am, and report to wardrobe (usually the back of a truck with a gondola) after checking
in, depending on whether or not you're an extra or a principal
you may or may not report to make up. The majority of the day
is the crew putting things together and taking them apart. So
when you arrive the crew has already shown up had breakfast
and are already setting up. If your call time is 5am, I promise
you the crew got there much, much sooner.

Once you're checked in and wardrobe has approved you, you
will go to the wait area. If you're union your area may be separate from those who are non-union. If you're principal, you
may be shown to your trailer. The assistant director will pull
the actors she needs based on the scene they're shooting.

Television vs. Film vs. Commercials

Television could provide steady employment provided it sur-
vives the pilot and test audience. Depending on the show, most

shows run for several seasons providing a lucrative income for those involved. In the beginning there were only three ABC, CBS, and NBC, and later PBS, now there's TBS, TNT, Disney Channel, Nickelodeon, The History Channel, the Soap Network and USA network, just to name a few.

The cool thing about television is that you see the same people day after day, cast and crew become like family. If you prove yourself reliable (come to work on time, follow directions, keep a good attitude) they will call you back, and if you're good at what you do you may find yourself in more shots, and maybe get bumped up to a speaking role.

A film shoot can take up to six weeks give or take, the good thing is that it can end up on the big screen which means big exposure and huge opportunity, then its off to the next audition, or waiting for the next phone call from your agent.

When you think of film you think of Hollywood, and with all the sound stages and CGI (Computer Generated Image) there's hardly any reason to leave Los Angeles. The good news is directors will leave Hollywood to go on location, so if the story takes place in Seattle then they may pull talent from Seattle.

Most principal actors will be flown in from Hollywood, but the extra talent will be local, not to mention there are several major working studios outside Hollywood, Screen Gems for example is located in Wilmington, North Carolina. There's a Universal Studios located in Orlando. Although Orlando is known as a family vacation spot, Florida it self has had several major pictures shot there; The Punisher was shot in Tampa, Bad Boys was shot in Miami. Next to Los Angeles, New York is also a major spot for motion picture.

This is where it begins for most screen actors. PSA (Public Service Announcements) Local grocers, restaurants, places that attract a lot of tourist are going to run commercials all year round such as Orlando, Florida which has a huge commercial market because of Disney, Sea World, and Universal Studios, Charleston, SC with its Historic tours and sites, Atlanta Georgia and any other city that has a Six Flags Amusement Park. All these places want to attract tourist so all those mentioned will run national ads, local venues will run state or regional ads.

Still commercial training is going to be different from film and television training. Depending on what you want to do will depend on the type of training you want to get.

As an extra the pay is usually a small sum, any where between $75 and $300 give or take but as principal you receive not only a larger sum, but residuals for as long as the commercial runs, you'll receive pay every quarter. Some actors are lucky enough to live on their residuals and not have to worry about working a 9 to 5. For actors that don't receive residuals must find another way to supplement their income until the next gig,...more on that later.

Generally you will be working an 8 hour day, but sometimes you may run in to over time. Principal actors tend to put in 12 hours, especially if voiceovers are needed. Here is what you can expect, in screen acting there's a lot of hurry up and wait. You may arrive at 5:00am but they may not need you until

11:00am, you'll break for lunch at 12:00pm, but if you end up working a full day most likely you'll be fed twice.

Union vs. Non-union

Earlier I said that there were two types of actors, those with speaking roles and those without. There's also union and non-union. Union or SAG Screen Actor's Guild will command a higher rate of pay and better working conditions when it comes to breaks, meals, and dressing room facilities. I once arrived on the set of a commercial where two tents were set up, one marked union and the other marked non-union. I honestly don't know the difference because the same beverages as far as I could see that were provided for union were also provided for the non-union.

Principal actors especially those with house hold names, will have a private dressing room or trailer, and extras will be corralled into one big greenroom or tent if filming outside.

When it comes to union the question often asked is; to be or not to be? If you are in L.A, and you are eligible it is worth it, but if your not in L.A, not traveling to L.A on a regular basis, there may be more non-union jobs available there fore limiting yourself in the job market.

First unit vs. Second unit

In action films and television shows there are two units; the first unit shoots the principal actors, and the second unit shoots the stunt sequence.

The first unit shoots the principal actors, so the established shot, close ups and reactions shoots are going to be shot, so we're talking at least 5 shots of the same scene, not to mention the retakes every time someone forgets a line. So expect to shoot the same scene over and over again.

The second unit, which I find to be the most exciting, may or may not have the principal actors in the scene, in fact they are most likely to have may have stunt doubles, and stunt actors. A stunt double is a look a like of the principal actor that does the stunt work. A stunt double is an actor that specializes in stunt work, these are the people that fall out of buildings in place of the principal actor. The stunt actor generally play henchmen to the antagonist, the irony is though you may hate them on screen, in real life they're some of the coolest people to hang with.

CHAPTER THREE
AUDITIONS

Generally for a role as an extra you agree to show up, hang out in the crowd and get paid. But if you are called for a speaking role you may have to audition.

Auditions tend to go like this: generally the characters are already typed, meaning female blond hair, blue eyes, and slender build. Understand that if this is you, there will be 40 others just like you trying out for the same role, what you have to do is perform outstanding in your screen test.

Because the entertainment business has grown, many colleges and universities have developed not only theatre programs, that not only teach acting, but the technicalities that go with it.

Even better, because of the major motion pictures that have been filmed and continued to be filmed in Florida, many colleges here have developed a film program where students often get to write, direct, and produce their own films, so they are constantly casting for student films. This means there is work available and opportunity to gain work and experience. Most important thing to remember, most major directors today were student film makers at one time.

More often than not, you will have to audition for the role you want to play, so here are some audition tips.

* When going to an audition you should always try to look your best.

* Your headshots should look the way you look when you hand them to the casting director. if the head is clean shaven, you should be as well. If you've cut your hair since your last photo shoot, then you should consider redoing your headshot or wait until your hair grows back before going to another audition.

* You should make sure that your headshots are professional standard size and color for television and film auditions, black and white for theatre.

* Your resume should be securely attached to the back of your headshot. Try to limit it to one page, and don't worry if your experience is limited.

* Name and phone number is all that's required as far as contact information is concerned, but for your security do not include your home address.

* Never lie on your resume.

* Many auditions may require a cold reading, but it doesn't hurt to have a monologue prepared.

AUDITIONING FOR A COLD READ

I've gone to auditions where the sides (lines) have been emailed to me a day or two ahead of time, but there were also times when I've walked into a cold read as well. A cold read is when you walk into an audition and see the script for the first time, in fact some agencies require you to read for them before sending you out on an audition. Before I tell you what a cold read is let me tell you what it isn't; it is not to see how well you read, or how proficient you can read, but to see how well you interpret the script.

When you go in to do a cold read you will be given the script or sides when you arrive and given a little bit of time to read it over just before you audition, no one expects you to mind read and give exactly what they're looking for but you are expected to give some choices, and ask some questions. Once the questions are answered you will begin.

After your read, the casting director may say "okay let me see something different" hopefully you would have made another choice or way to interpret the character. After a second read she may say "could you maybe try reading it like this?" just to see if you can follow directions, or she just may say "Thank you for coming."

TRAINING

Classes and work shops can increase your chances of nailing the audition. You may have landed the staring role in all your high school plays, but this isn't high school, this is the real world and the competition is stiff.

Training doesn't guarantee a role but it does help. The type of training you receive depends greatly on the market you're in. Respectively, the training you receive in theatre may not be adequate for television and film, for that I recommend that you take an "acting for camera" class.

Most legitimate acting for camera classes are taught by some-one who has been in the business, such as a former or current actor or a former or current film or casting directors who have been successful in their field and have the reputation and cre-dentials to prove it. Acting for camera and acting for stage re-quires different techniques for example;

Acting for Camera:

* Movement is smaller.

* Audio will pick up you voice

* Are usually shot out of sequence

* You may not have time to get to know the person, only the character they portray.

* Expression is internalized

Acting for Stage:

* Movement is larger

* Voice must be projected

* Is performed for a live audience from beginning to end

* You spend more time getting to know your cast

* Expression is large and exaggerated

Not only is there a difference in acting techniques from stage to screen, but the technique from commercials acting and television and film as well, and just as there are different genres in television and film, there are different genres in commercials too.

CHAPTER FOUR
LEGAL STUFF

This chapter is devoted to some the legal stuff that goes on with becoming a screen actor such as contracts, unions, pay, residuals and perpetuity, let's start with contracts.

CONTRACTS

A contract is a binding agreement between two or more people. Contracts are negotiated so that each person entering the agreement can understand the working conditions and the rate of pay. For the actor and his/her agent the contract is a written document that will state how long the relationship will last between parties and the percentage of pay the agent will receive.

For the actor and the production company the contract is a written document that will state how long the relationship will last between parties involved and how much the production company agrees to pay the actor, which is usually negotiated between the production company and the actor's agent.

Contracts can be tricky, legal jargon isn't exactly the easiest language to understand, but in this chapter I hope to make things a little easier for you. When it comes to contracts there are a few terms you need to know. The first one I learned was non-exclusive. First of all, no matter what you decide to do in life, do not sign a contract without reading it, and do not sign or allow yourself to be pressured into signing a contract if you do not understand the terms and conditions of the contract,

even if its a `Once in a lifetime opportunity". If you don't un-
derstand its better to ask attorney to review the contract and
explain the contents to you.

The first contract you come across may be your agency's contract. That was the first contract I had to sign, a two year non-
exclusive contract. A non-exclusive contract means that you
are not bound or limited to the one agency, but are free to work
with several other agencies at once. Signing an exclusive contract can limit you.

Understand that policy may change from company to company
and market to market. I know in my last book (How to become
a Professional Screen Actor and or Model in Florida, iuniverse
publishing 2007) I said that if someone wants you sign an exclusive contract, walk away. That is the case with Florida, but
it may not be the case with Los Angeles. In Florida there isn't
nearly as much work as there is in Los Angeles, so if you live
in Florida most agencies understand that you really can't afford
to tie yourself down to just one agency, although you may
come across some that will try to hold you exclusively, in that
case you will have to make a judgment call.

The other contract, as I said before, is between you and the
production company which states the length of time you will be
working and the amount of pay you will receive. Then there's
Perpetuity.

PERPETUITY

Perpetuity generally refers to commercials. Perpetuity is when a company or entity owns your image forever and can use it for any reason they see fit, with out further compensation other than initial payment. This is usually perpetrated by large corporations with deep pockets that can afford to compensate you but don't want to. Here's the catch, if you are offered a role from their competitor it will be considered a conflict of interest and must be turned down, if not, you can be sued, and here's why;

Perpetuity says that if your image appears in a commercial for Company D, then you may not appear in a commercial for Company B, if they operate the same type of business. For example, if you do a commercial for a sea food chain, then you're not allowed to do one for it's competition. The same goes for theme parks, grocery chains and so on and so forth. That makes sense, if I was running a business I'd expect the same, but now here is where it gets ugly. Company D has the right to use your image for rest of your natural life "without compensation" in any ad they see fit for any duration of time, and so now you have a decision to make. I can't tell you what that is because its really up to you.

THE UNION

The Screen Actors Guild or SAG is the union that represents more than 100,000 members across the United States.

The purpose of SAG is not only to negotiate, but enforce contracts for professional performers in film, television, commercials, music and interactive videos. This organization gives you collective strength and power of the acting community.

The headquarters is located in Los Angeles, but this union has offices throughout the United States. The union improves working conditions, enhances compensation, and other benefits.

Understand that being in the union is not a requirement, and not everyone is eligible. There is one important thing to note. Whether or not you're a member of the guild, you should not accept work when the guild is on strike.

To SAG or not to SAG that is the question. If you are non-union and you live in …lets say the Orlando area then you can audition for SAG and non-SAG jobs, but if you're SAG you can only audition for and except SAG jobs which are few and far between outside of Los Angeles.

If you live in the Los Angeles or New York Area it only makes sense to join, since almost all the work is SAG, if not, joining SAG could be detrimental to your career. For qualifying information go to the SAG website.

Please mail your document to:
Screen Actors Guild

Membership Services Department – Proof of Eligibility

5757 Wilshire Blvd.

Los Angeles, CA 90036

PAY

Getting paid for a production company has its similarities and differences from a regular 9 to 5. Your taxes are taken out just like any other job, but at the same time don't expect your check to come in the mail by the next week. Sometimes you'll get your check the following week and other times you'll get your check the following month sometimes longer. This is why a lot of actors as well as other artist have supplemental income.

Your agent gets 10%, but as you get to know people, there may come a time when a casting director may call you directly at home. Some now may even contact you through myspace, facebook or some other social internet site. If that's the case then you keep the entire check, unless your agency contract dictates otherwise.

The extra casting companies that I spoke of in the first chapter do not require 10% of your pay, because they're not agents.

The rate of pay can vary from state to state, it's no secret that rates are cheaper out side of Los Angeles, especially for non-union.

RESIDUALS
Residuals is the pay you receive after the commercial has aired, as long as a commercial (usually national) is aired, you get paid every time it airs.

In any case if there is something in a contract you do not understand you should ask, and if you still have doubt by all means ask an entertainment attorney.

CHAPTER FIVE
PRINT WORK
The Steps to Modeling

Getting into modeling or Print Work, as its known in the industry, follows similar steps when starting out, you may get discovered in the mall but it's highly unlikely. Like acting there are steps you should follow that are the same and yet different. You should still seek an agent, and you should still hire a professional photographer simply for this; Actors leave head shots, Models leave composite cards. Some leave both, especially when starting out.

Models who do print work are the actors and models you see in the Sears® or JC Penny catalogue or the print ads in the news paper. The students you see in text books, they're getting paid for that, supplementing their income.

The steps to print work really aren't that much different from becoming an actor. Before I gave you the steps to acting, I will now give you the steps to modeling;

STEP ONE: HIRE A PROFES-
SIONAL PHOTOGRAPHER

Preferably the same one you hired for your headshots, unless for some reason you were not happy with the last one, ask around and find another one. You will also need to bring several different sets of attire. The photographer is going to take hundreds of photographs, the last thing you need is hundreds of photos with you in the same outfit. That would be a waste of time and money.

Agencies want to see you in different types of clothing, so you want to compose a different number of looks, such as casual, business casual, swim wear, underwear. You may want to consult with the photographer who's been in the business and see what they recommend.

When you consider the hundreds of catalogs out there, not to mention all the stores in the malls, and mall outlets, there are dozens of looks to consider. At least one of them is you, for example; If you're athletically built, then perhaps you could model for Sports Authority, let's face it, the person that models for Gap probably won't be the person that models golf wear.

Step Two: You need Composite

Your photographer is most likely capable of putting together the composite for you. A professional is well aware of what you need and therefore may include this in their packet, or bill you separately as an additional service at extra cost. If not then you may take your photos to 'Photo Scan' in Orlando. This is the best and most reliable place to get duplications of your composites, and they are reasonably priced.

Photo Scan is located at 646 Bryn Mawr St. the number to call is (407) 839-5029, from Hwy. 50 drive north on Edge Water Dr., then take a right on Bryn Mawr Street. Their hours are 10:00 am to 5:00 p.m.

Sarah Mendes

Central Florida Talent
(407) 930-9226 Fax (407) 830-4610

Height: 5'6" • **Weight:** 110 • **Hair:** Brown • **Eyes:** Brown
Dress Size: 4-6 • **Bust:** 34 • **Waist:** 26 • **Hips:** 37½ • **Shoe:** 6½
D.O.B.: Dec. 2, 1985

This is the perfect example of a composite

STEP THREE: FIND AN AGENT

I'm not going to repeat myself about the whole agency thing. In the Reference section I have listed some of the most reliable as well as legitimate talent agencies in Florida. They will call you when someone seeks your talent. It is up to you whether or not you want to take the job, but if you decide to take the job, you must be reliable. Show up for your call time on time, do what is lawfully asked of you while on set, and pay the agency their 20% on time.

PHOTO TIPS:

The first tip I'm going to give you is simple, be on time. The photographer has other appointments, and running behind on your schedule is going to cause him /her to run behind on other clients. If you are going to be late at least have the courtesy to call and let them know. If at all possible, please try to arrive early.

Here are some bullet points to get you started:

* Meet with your photographer prior to your session to discuss problems you've had with other photographers, and also to discuss wardrobe, and different types, or looks you may want to portray, especially if you're doing composites.

* If you're getting headshots, try not to draw attention away from your face by wearing patterns.

* If you have small children with you, please make arrangements for someone to keep watch over them. Since Florida is such a family attraction, you may want to include them in your photo.

* Please don't bring anyone or anything that may be a distraction.

* Please bring your clothes clean, ironed, and on hangers.

* Arrive with a clean face if you are having your make up done at the studio, this includes mascara.

* If you're doing your own makeup arrive early with every-thing you need such as hairspray, or powder.

* Please do not show up with your hair wet or dirty.

* If you have pierced ears studs are best for headshots, for composites you can wear pretty much anything.

* Arriving in a ponytail can be a bad idea since combing out the kinks may take time.

* If it matters to you, bring your own music.

* If you have any special request such as a rush on proofs or prints, let your photographer know ahead of time so that he/she can accommodate you.

* If you are taking photos for composites and your photographer is able to do this make sure that you do not place the same look in all three photos, remember you want different looks: business, business casual, swim suit, etc.

* Second most important even though I saved it for last, get a good nights sleep so that you may arrive on time, fresh, and with a positive attitude.

Remember these photos are your calling card, so you want t look your best and feel great. How you feel will come across in the photos, if you feel great, you'll look great. If you feel crappy, you'll look crappy; your photo session is what you make it, so make the best of it.

CHAPTER SIX
SUPPLEMENTAL INCOME

If you have not yet established yourself in the industry you are or will become a starving artist if you don't find a way to supplement your income. If you don't live in Hollywood there may be little to no production going on in your area, therefore you need to find another way to supplement your income. It feels good to be working; but what happens when you wrap?

In between you need to have income coming in, and commercials, industrials, print work, and stage are some ways to do it. If acting is what you want, working a regular 9 to 5 isn't really going to help you. Its highly unlikely that your boss is going to be supportive of you taking extra time off to go to auditions, or film shoots, so you need a job that's going to be flexible with your schedule, so here are some ways to make money in between television, film and commercial jobs;

INDUSTRIALS

Industrials are used in training and show case. If you've ever worked for a fast food restaurant and had to watch a training video, this would be an industrial. If you've ever stayed in a resort, some have a channel that only talks exclusively about the resort 24 hours a day, seven days a week, this would also be an industrial.

TELE-PROMPTING

Tele-prompting is reading out loud, You may have seen the in-fomercials and home shopping network, those are all tele-prompters and I hear the pay is quite nice. If you're in between productions, tele-prompting isn't a bad way to supplement your income.

VOICE OVER

Voice over is the stuff you hear on the radio, long before the film and television actor there was the radio actor, they were the pioneers for what we do today. Before television was invented families would gather around the radio to tune in to their favorite programs, today radio actors are mainly used for advertising.

There is training for that and if you're interested I suggest that you seek training.

SUBSTITUTE TEACHER

Substitute teacher is not related to the acting industry, but it's the one job I know of with the most flexibility which leaves you open for auditions and gigs. In other words, its not a job that you're required to report to monday through friday from 9 to 5.

Requirements for substitute teacher vary from state to state, and sometimes county to county within the state. In one state or county you'll need a high school diploma, but the next county or state over may require 2 years of college or 60 credits equivalent. For example California requires not only a 4 year degree, but a passing score on their C-BEST exam.

Just like requirements a substitute teacher salary varies from state to state and county to county. On average a substitute teacher can make $50 to $200 per day, give or take. Some consider substitute teaching the worst job, everyone knows how the substitute is treated, by the students as well as the faculty and staff depending on what school you're working at.

The advantage is that you get to pick and choose the days, and schools you want to work unless you're a permanent sub for a school then you have to go in everyday just like everybody else. As a regular sub you never have to worry about asking for the day off.

The disadvantage is that you are paid less than a regular teacher, and you are offered no benefits. Sometimes you'll receive little or no respect from students, or teachers, and sometimes little support from administration, but then you're not a teacher you're an actor, and this is only supplemental income, just money to get you buy until the next gig.

TAXI DRIVER

Taxi Drivers are a lot like substitute teachers, no set schedule. They often work when they want as long as they want, as long as they make enough to pay back the cab company for the use of the car. Different requirements will most likely vary where ever you go.

CHAPTER SEVEN
Tips for the Stage Mom

In theatre, a 40 year old woman could probably get away with playing the part of red riding hood on a stage production, but I doubt if she could get away with that on television or film. In television and film art often imitates life, and people want to see the role of a child portrayed by a child. So how does a parent get their child started in this business? First, make sure it's something they want to do, if you're reading this, then perhaps you've already established that.

For children, the guidelines are pretty much the same, child labor laws may apply, if the child gets frequent work say maybe a sitcom or series, many working studios have teachers on set for the working child actors. However, if you decide to home school, be sure to register with the State or your affiliate home school report. If it's just here and there a meeting with the teacher or school principal might be helpful. In my experience you sometimes get a call from your agent the night before so it helps to have a teacher or principal who's sensitive to your needs.

Helping your child follow their dream is the best thing a parent can do, enough said, here are some helpful tips if you are looking to get your child in the business;

* First make sure this is something he/she wants, I would hate to think that someone would use this to live vicariously through their child.

* It's going to be a long day, plan for it bring snacks, games, homework, enough to keep you busy for twelve hours.

* Sometimes they feed you, sometimes they don't, be prepared.

* Keep copies of your child's birth certificate, social security card, and keep extra head shots and or composite cards on you. It may be wise to put together a special binder with these items.

* Do not leave your child unsupervised on any set for any reason. Make sure that you or someone you trust is present at all times. They must be supervised by you or a legally appointed guardian.

Understand that this is more than just an extra curriculum, this could be the start of your child's career if they're ready. So how do you know if they're ready? Children are not shy when it comes to expressing interest in what they want. They may ask to join a drama group at school or just put on a production right in your living room. If that's the case start small, go with an extra casting company, start out with extra work, and training.

You also may want to open a minors savings account in their name at your bank or local credit union simply because checks are going to come in their name.

CHAPTER EIGHT
CONCLUSION

When I was in school, they taught us how to write essays. There is a formula to it; tell them what you're going to tell them, tell them, and in the conclusion tell them what you told them. That's how most conclusions are written, "tell them what you told them." Well, I'm not going to do that, instead I'm going to give you something useful to take with you.

First I'm going to recommend that you read the following books; *How not to audition* by Ellie Kanner and Denny Martin Flinn, and *How to make a living as a Working actor in L.A.* by Michael-John Wolfe, and *Resumes for Performing Arts Careers* from the Editors of VGM Career Books.

Second, I'm going to give you some last minute tips;

* Keep your cell phone charged with your agents number programed on speed dial.

* Keep two separate wardrobes just for working, keep them pressed and ready to go in a garment bag so that you're not scrambling at the last minute. One for commercial work and one for Television and film. If its print work the wardrobe will most likely be picked out for you.

* Keep a binder with extra copies of head shot, resumes and composites, and copies of your social security card and or birth certificate if the actor is under the age of 18.

* Speaking of age, if you're 18 or older, never put your age or date of birth on your head shots or composites.

Last I'm going to tell you that you are responsible for your career, not your agent, and not your manager, be that as it may, your success often depends largely on the people and situations you surround yourself with.

I think everyone has someone or something in their life, intentionally or unintentionally that could potentially hold them back. It could be where you live, it could be a jealous relative or a jealous lover, or friend, worst of all, it could be you if you let them and your situation get inside your head. Some of us are able to over come it and some of us allow ourselves to get caught up.

When you find success in whatever you decide to do, and I hope you do, don't expect anyone you know to be happy for you, some will, most won't. When you land that first commercial, or role that's when you'll find out who your real friends are, and this may or may not cause some restructuring in your life.

There are plenty of people you probably know who have dreams but aren't doing anything about it, but the minute you try to follow your dream, some may try to discourage you, and they will if you let them.

If you succeed in spite of them, they will declare that you've changed, or you sold out. Some will tell you to your face that you're trying to be something you're not, some may even use religion to cause you to question you're morality, or tell you you're not good enough and the rest will just talk behind your back. If you listen long enough you start to doubt yourself and believe that you aren't worthy especially if your being rejected in every audition you go to. Maybe it's none of that maybe where you live there's no commercial market or major production.

This is where life management comes into play, and for that I say surround yourself with positive people, believe in yourself, go where the money is, but most of all stay focused and don't get distracted. Now, if this subject was on any other career I would say good luck, but its not, so I'll just say, break a leg.

REFERENCE

PHOTOGRAPHERS
CALIFORNIA

ALDEN PHOTOGRAPHY
5555 Olive Lane
North Hollywood, California 91601
United States
P: 818 766-2919
Fax: 818 766-2919
email: coolhandkory@hotmail.com

JAMAL BAYETTE PHOTOGRAPHY
30 Dudley Ave #2
Venice, California 90291
United States
P: 310 450 1365
email: jamal@jamalbayette.com

CALAS STUDIO
450 1/2 N. Hayworth Ave
Los Angeles, California 90048
United States
P: 213-804-3116
email: headshots@calasstudio.com

KEELAN CHEZA PHOTOGRAPHY
10621 Regent St Suite 1
Los Angeles, California 90034
United States
P: 310.559.8075
Fax: 310.559.8085

email: keelan@silverdoor.net

PIERRE COMTOIS PHOTOGRAPHY
P.O. Box 48166
Los Angeles, California 90048
United States
P: 323.251.5593
email: pierre@pierrecomtoisphotography.com

DMN PHOTO
Los Angeles, California 90066
United States
P: 310-567-9045
email: info@dmnphoto.com

KENNETH DOLIN PHOTOGRAPHY
311 N. Robertson Blvd. #536
Beverly Hills, California 90211
United States
P: (310) 429-2876
email: kennethdolin@earthlink.net

FOTOLOGY L.A
10629 Woodbridge #106
Toluca Lake, California 91602
United States
P: 818-640-8173
email: david@fotology-la.com

RETO HALME PHOTOGRAPHY
1818 N. Whitley Ave #300
Hollywood, California 90028
United States

P: 917-770-2408
email: reto@reto-photography.com

ANGIE HILL PHOTOGRAPHY
P.O. Box 66952
Los Angeles, California 90069
United States
P: 323-309-6314
email: missangiehill@gmail.com

ROBIN HOLLYWOOD PHOTOGRAPHY
Los Angeles, California
United States
P: 818-259-2129
email: robinhollywood@robinhollywood.com

KAARINA PHOTOGRAPHY
2368 North Alvarado Street
Los Angeles, California 90039
United States
P: 310 497-2165
email: keaufranc@yahoo.com

KURTY PHOTOGRAPHY
1759 47th Avenue
San Francisco, California 94122
United States
P: 415-566-9500
email: kurty@kurtyphotography.com

JO LIU PHOTOGRAPHY
1308 Factory Place #204
Los Angeles, California 90013

United States
P: 213-623-2556
email: jo@joliuphotography.com

JULIET LOFARO PHOTOGRAPHS
129 W. 29th Street
New York, New York 10001
United States
P: 212-643-1123
email: info@julietlofaro.com

JOE LYMAN PHOTOGRAPHY
8304 Atlanta #105
Huntington Beach, California 92646
United States
P: 714-969-3053
email: joelymanphoto@netscape.net

WES McDOWELL PHOTOGRAPHY
Hollywood, California 90046
United States
P: 310-770-0230
email: photobywes@aol.com

CHRISTOPHER NOLAN
Christophernoland.com
2212 North Cahuenga Blvd.
Hollywood Hills, California 90068
(310) 388-7230
chris@christophernoland.com

TAILI PHOTOGRAPHY
79-010 Via San Clara

La Quinta, California 92253
United States
P: 323 663-0880
email: taili@tailiphoto.com

THIRD-I-PHOTO
5250 Denny Ave# 203
North Hollywood, California 91601
United States
P: 818-508-5897
email: jnewcomb@thirdiphoto.com

THIRD-I-PHOTO
4627 Tilden Ave #3
Sherman Oaks, California 91403
United States
P: 8187957368
email: thirdiphoto@yahoo.com

KEN WEINGART PHOTOGRAPHY
204 Washington Ave. #108
Santa Monica, California 90403
United States
P: 310 395-4613
email: info@kenweingart.com

FLORIDA

ORLANDO HEADSHOTS
www.orlandoheadshots.com

email: mail@orlandoheadshots.com
P: (407) 925-6235

SEAN L. BREWER PHOTOGRAPHY
(407) 310-7484
www.seanbrewerimages.com
Email: seanlbrewer@aol.com

TIM TEW PHOTOGRAPHY
600 N. Boundary #106-A
Deland, Florida 32720
(386)748-3592
www.studiotew.com

TRUDYELLEN PHOTOGRPHY (South Florida)
5883 Bartram Street
Boca Raton, Florida 33433
United States
P: 5613478783
email: trudyellen@msn.com

WET ORANGE STUDIOS, INC.
5530 Hansel Ave.
Orlando. Florida 32809
(407) 240-6505
www.michaelcarins.com

PHOTO SCAN (Photo duplication, not a photographer)
646 Bryn Mawr Street
Orlando, Florida
(407) 839-5029
Open from 10:00 a.m. to 5:00 p.m.
www.ggphotoscan.com

MASSACHUSETTS

VALARIE SEABROOK PHOTOGRAPHER
221 Mass. Ave Studio 911
Boston, Massachusetts 02115
United States
P: 617-236-2256
Fax: 617-236-2256
email: valarie.seabrook@verizon.net

MISSOURI

ANGIE KNOST PHOTOGRAPHY
8039 Watson Rd. Suite 150
Webster Groves, Missouri 63119
United States
P: 314-963-9981
email: angieknostphoto@hotmail.com

ANGIE KNOST PHOTOGRAPHY (Mailing address)
PO Box 190474
St. Louis, Missouri 63119
United States
P: 314-253-2838
email: angieknostphoto@hotmail.com

NEW JERSEY

AARON SEALS PHOTOGRAPHY
95 Prospect Street
Lodi, New Jersey 07644

United States
P: 914.620.4150
email: photo212@aol.com

NEW YORK

CHARLES BRONSTEIN
2 Lincoln Square
New York, New York 10025
United States
P: 917-788-9004
email: lgrisez@lemel.fr

JIM BULGATZ PHOTOGRAPHY
145 West 67th St., #33e
New York, New York 10023
United States
P: 646-220-6969
email: jbulgatz@nyc.rr.com

ARTHUR COHEN PHOTOGRAPHY
56 West 22nd St. 8th Floor
New York, New York 10010
United States
P: 212-691-5244
Fax: 212-691-5256
email: arthur@arthurcohen.com

EVAN COHEN PHOTOGRAPHY
39 west 14th street
suite 501
New York, New York 10011
United States

P: 212 242-0350
Fax: 212 242-0350
email: evan@evancohenstudio.com

GAVIN ELLIOT PHOTOGRAPHY
New York, New York 10011
United States
P: 609 203 7403
email: lance.krieger@sharedfamilyoffice.com

FATCHETT PHOTOGRAPHY
New York City, New York
United States
P: 212.875.7599
email: photo@fatchett.com

KEVIN FOX PHOTOGRAPHY
515 Greenwich St #502
New York, New York 10012
United States
P: 646-431-0214
email: Kevin@FoxPhotography.net

ROD GOODMAN PHOTOGRAPHER
45 Wall Street suite 1612
New York, New York 10005-1919
United States
P: 212.929.1654
email: photosbyrod@earthlink.net

JOE HENSON PHOTOGRAPHY
236 West 27th Street

Suite 10RW
New York, New York 10001
United States
P: 212-463-0575
Fax: 212-463-0608
email: joe@joehenson.com

PETER HURLEY PHOTOGRAPHY
601 W 26th Street, Suite 1425E
New York, New York 10001
United States
P: 212.627.2210
Fax: 801 681-1464
email: sessions@peterhurley.com

INFOCUS GRAPHICS, INC.
44 E. 21st street
New York, New York 10010
United States
P: 212-674-3067
Fax: 212-677-6478
email: brad@infocusgraphicsny.com

WILLIAM JAMES PHOTOGRAPHY
New York City, New York 10019
United States
P: 212-586-9351
email: wjames5@nyc.rr.com

LISA-MARIE PHOTOGRAPHY
20 East 33rd St
New York, New York 10016
United States

P: 212-340-4619
email: lmmazzucco@optonline.net

ALEX KAPLAN HEADSHOTS & MODEL PORTFOLIO
SPECIALIST
Upper West Side
New York City, New York 10024
United States
P: 917-992-9097
email: alex@professionalheadshots.com

BETH KELLY PHOTOGRAPHY
265 W. 30th street
New York City, New York 10010
United States
P: 212 868 1604
email: Emily@bethkellyphotography

LUCILLE KHORNAK
425 East 58th Street
New York, New York 10022
United States
P: 212-593-0933
email: lucille@lucillekhornak.com

PETER KONERKO PHOTOGRAPHY
33 Washington Street
DUMBO
Brooklyn, New York 11201
United States
P: 718-858-4589
email: contact@peterkonerko.com

BRENT KRAUSE PHOTOGRAPHY
200 West 79th street
New York, New York 10018
United States
P: 917-494-1561
email: brentakrause@hotmail.com

CHRIS MACKE PHOTOGRAPHY
Midtown - New York City
New York, New York 10036
United States
P: 1-877-833-4949
Fax: 1-877-833-4949
email: email@mackephotography.com

JIM MILLER PHOTOGRAPHY
343 West 21 Street
New York, New York 10011
United States
P: 212 691 4029
email: jimmiller.photo@verizon.net

NEW YORK HEADSHOTS
302 Bedford Ave
Suite# 297
Brooklyn, New York 11211
United States
P: 347.276.0211
email: info@new-york-headshots.com

GLENN OFFLEY PHOTOGRAPHY
402 Vanderbilt Ave
3rd Floor

Brooklyn, New York 11238
United States
P: 718.399.0505
Fax: 718.399.3195
email: glenn0005@hotmail.com

ANTON OPARIN PHOTOGRAPHY / CastWeb.com
244 Fifth Avenue
Suite 2023
New York, New York 10001
United States
P: (917) 815-1113
Fax: (212) 202-4060
email: simc@castweb.com

GARVEY RICH
256 East 10th Street
New York, New York 10009
United States
P: 917 450 4856
email: garvoir@weareallgurus.com

NORTH CAROLINA

MARK FORTENBERRY PHOTOGRAPHY
2171 Hawkins Street
Charlotte, North Carolina 28203
United States
P: 704-342-4454
Fax: 704-342-0404
email: mark@fortenberryphoto.com

THE PHOTOGRAPHY PLACE

10915-A Monroe Road
Matthews, North Carolina 28105
United States
P: 704-708-8424
Fax: 704-708-8905
email: wwshooter@msn.com

OREGON

MICHAEL D. CLINE PHOTOGRAPHY
P.O. Box 3114
Salem, Oregon 97302
United States
P: (503)362-7140
email: info@michaelcline.com

PENNSYLVANIA

SOFIA NEGRON - PHOTOGRAPHER
3636 Cresson Street
Philadelphia, Pennsylvania 19127
United States
P: 215-327-8482
email: sofianegron@yahoo.com

TENNESSEE

STEPHEN L. BRYANT PHOTOGRAPHY WORLD WIDE
P. O. Box 2995
Murfreesboro, Tennessee 37133-2995
United States
P: (615) 585-1300
email: mrpeterrmiller@hotmail.com

TEXAS

BRIAKAUFF PRODUCTIONS
PO Box 92165
Austin, Texas 78709
United States
P: 512-301-1706
Fax: 512-301-1706
email: jbrian@briakauff.com

WASHINGTON

MELISSA O'HEARN
Seattle, Washington 98112
United States
P: 206.276.5170
email: melissa.ohearn@gmail.com

TALENT AGENCIES

ALABAMA

ACT PRODUCTIONS (America's Choice Talent)
Modeling Agency
Hueytown, AL 35023
(205) 491-3205
(205) 491-3064

ALABAMA TALENT & MODEL MGMT.

Tuscaloosa, AL 35402
205-364-8700
Fax: 205-364-8813
E-mail: Altalent@altavista.com

SUZANNE T MASSINGILL
Agency Director
Barefoot Models & Talent
Mobile, Alabama
Phone: 251-344-5554
Web: www.barefootagency.com

BEAU MONDE PRODUCTIONS UNLIMITED INC.
Montgomery, AL 36116
(334) 286-3696

CATHI LARSEN AGENCY
Birmingham, AL 35210
(205) 951-2445

CYNTHIA'S STUDIO MODEL & TALENT AGENCY
Montgomery, AL 36106
(334) 272-5555
(334) 262-8755

IMAGES UNLIMITED
Anniston, AL 36201
(205) 236-0952

KIDDIN' AROUND/REAL PEOPLE
Birmingham, AL 35233
(205) 323-KIDS 5437 (Make-up Wagons)

MARIE PRATER
Birmingham, AL 35226
(205) 822-8135
Fax: (205) 979-0912

RARE QUALITY MODELS & TALENT
Montgomery, AL 36117
(334) 244-4464

STAR QUALITY TALENT AGENCY
Decatur, AL 35601
(205) 353-0773

HAMILTON MODEL & TALENT AGENCY
Huntsville, AL 35805
(205) 517-5072
Pager: (205) 351-3485
Fax: (205) 517-5073

SVI TALENT AGENCY
P.O. Box 339
Trussville, Alabama 35173
Web: www.sviagency.com
E-mail: sviagency@yahoo.com

WINDHAM ENTERTAINMENT, INC.
1931 Woodmore Drive
Huntsville, AL 35803
Phone: (256) 489-8080
Web: http://www.windhamentertainment.com

CALIFORNIA

AGENCY FOR PERFORMING ARTS
9200 Sunset Blvd, Suite 900
Hollywood, CA 90069
(310)273-0744

AFFINITY Model & Talent Agency, Inc.
8721 Santa Monica Blvd. Suite #27
West Hollywood, CA 90069-4511
Tel: 323-525-0577
Fax: 323-843-9696
Web: www.affinitytalent.com

ARTIST MANAGEMENT TALENT AGENCY
835 Fifth Avenue, Suite #411
San Diego, CA 92101
(619)233-6655

AMSEL, EISENSTADT, FRAZIER
5757 Wilshire #510
Los Angeles, CA 90036

THE ARTISTS GROUP
10100 Santa Monica Blvd #2490
Los Angeles, CA 90067

BAIER-KLEINMAN INTERNATIONAL
3575 West Cahuenga Blvd., Suite 500
Hollywood, CA 90068
(818)761-1001

BEVERLY HECHT AGENCY
12001 Ventura Pl #320
Studio City, CA 91604

BADGELEY CONNOR KING
9229 Sunset Blvd #311
Los Angeles, CA 90069

BALDWIN TALENT, INC,
8055 W. Manchester Ave.
Ste. 550
Playa del Rey, CA 90293
Phone: (310) 827-2422

BOOM MODELS & TALENT
2325 3rd Street, Suite #223
San Francisco, CA 94107
(415)626-6591

THE BLAKE AGENCY
415 N. Camden Drive, Suite #111,
Beverly Hills, CA 90210
(310)246-0241

CNA & ASSOCIATES, INC.,
1925 Century Park East, Suite #750
Hollywood, CA 90067
(310)556-4343

CACTUS TALENT AGENCY
13601 Ventura Boulevard, Suite #112
Sherman Oaks, CA 91423
(818)508-4894

COVERS MODEL & TALENT AGENCY
4716 Foulger Drive
Santa Rosa, CA 95405
(707)539-9252

BARBARA CAMERON & ASSOCIATES
8369 Sausalito Avenue, Suite A
West Hills, CA 91304
(818)888-6107

CAPITAL ARTISTS
8383 Wilshire Boulevard, Suite 954
Beverly Hills 90211
(310) 658-8118

COLOURS MODEL & TALENT MANAGEMENT AGENCY
8344 1/2 West Third Street
Hollywood, CA 90048
(310) 658-7072

CONTEMPORARY ARTISTS, LTD
1317 Fifth Street, Suite 200
Santa Monica, CA 90401
(310)395-1800

SUSAN CROW & ASSOCIATES
1010 Hammond Street, Suite #102
West Hollywood, CA 90069
(310)859-9784

DRAGON TALENT AND MODELS

8444 Wilshire Blvd
Penthouse Suite
Beverly Hills, CA 90211
323.653.0366
Web: www.dragontalent.com

ELEGANCE TALENT AGENCY
2763 State Street
Carlsbad, CA 92008
(760)434-3397

ENDEAVOR TALENT AGENCY, LLC
9701 Wilshire Blvd., 10th Floor
Beverly Hills, CA 90210
(310)248-2000

EVOLVE TALENT AGENCY
3435 Wilshire Bvld., Suite 2700
Los Angeles, CA 90010

FILM THEATRE ACTORS XCHNGE
582 Market St, Suite 302
San Francisco, CA 94104
(415)433-3920

FUTURE AGENCY
8929 S. Sepulveda Blvd., Suite 314
Hollywood, CA 90045
(310)338-9602

GENERATION MODEL & TALENT AGENCY
340 Brannan Street, Suite 302
San Francisco, CA 94107

(415)777-9099

HOWARD TALENT WEST
10657 Riverside Dr
Toluca Lake, CA 91602

HENDERSON/HOGAN AGENCY
247 S. Beverly Dr #102
Los Angeles, CA 90212

KELMAN/ARLETTA ASSOCIATES
7813 Sunset Blvd
Los Angeles, CA 90048

LOS ANGELES PREMIERE ARTISTS AGENCY
8899 Beverly Blvd., Suite 510
Hollywood, CA 90048
(310)271-1414

LOOK MODEL & TALENT AGENCY
166 Geary Blvd, Suite 1406
San Francisco, CA 94108
(415)781-2841

MITCHELL TALENT MANAGEMENT
323 Geary Street, Suite 302
San Francisco, CA 94102
(415)395-9475

PAKULA/KING AND ASSOC
9229 Sunset Blvd #315
Los Angeles, CA 90069

PANDA AGENCY
3721 Hoen Avenue
Santa Rosa, CA 95405
(707)576-0711

CLAUDIA QUINN ASSOCIATES
533 Airport Boulevard, Suite #400
Burlingame, CA 94010
(650)615-9950

SAN FRANCISCO TOP MODELS AND TALENT
870 Market Street, Suite 1076
San Francisco, CA 94102
(415)391-1800 (FS)

THE STARS AGENCY
777 Davis Street
San Francisco, CA 94111
(415)421-6272

MARLA DELL TALENT
2124 Union Street
San Francisco, CA 94123
(415)563-9213

DON SCHWARTZ ASSOCIATES
6922 Hollywood Blvd., Suite 508
Hollywood, CA 90028
(310) 464-4366

SAN DIEGO MODEL MANAGEMENT

438 Camino Del Rio South, Suite #116
San Diego, CA 92108
(619)296-1018

SCREEN ARTISTS AGENCY
12435 Oxnard Street,
North Hollywood, CA 91606
(818)755-0026

SELECT ARTISTS TALENT AGENCY
8439 Sunset Blvd., Suite 301
Hollywood, CA 90069
(310)654-2764

SHAPIRA & ASSOC
15301 Ventura Blvd, Suite 345
Sherman Oaks, CA 91403
(818)906-0322

SHAMON FREITAS & COMPANY
9606 Tierra Grande Street, Suite #204
San Diego, CA 92126
(858)549-3955
Web: http://www.shamonfreitas.com

TYLER KJAR AGENCY
5116 Lankershim Blvd
No Ho, CA 91601

UNITED TALENT AGENCY, INC
9560 Wilshire Blvd, 5th Floor
Beverly Hills, CA 90212
(310)273-6700

VISION ART MANAGEMENT
9200 Sunset Blvd., Penthouse 1
Hollywood, CA 90069
(310)888-3288

WORLD CLASS SPORTS
880 Apollo Street, Suite 337,
El Segundo, CA 90245
(310)535-9120

CARTER WRIGHT ENTERPRISES
6513 Hollywood Blvd, Suite 210
Hollywood, CA 90028
(310)469-0944

WRITERS AND ARTISTS AGENCY
924 Westwood Blvd., Suite 900
Los Angeles, CA 90024
(310)824-6300

P. ZEALOUS ARTISTS, INC
139 S. Beverly Drive, Suite 222
Beverly Hills, CA 90212
(310)281-3533

WALLIS AGENCY
1126 Hollywood Way #203-A
Burbank, CA 91505

DELAWARE

ZOM MANAGEMENT

PO Box 932
Bear, DE 19701
(302) 324-8885

TRICIA ALLEN
SHEKINAH MGMT.
P O Box 1307
Wilmington, DE 19899-1307
Phone: (302)325-2782
Fax: (302)324-8837
Web:
http://hometown.aol.com/shekinahde/myhomepage/index.ht
ml

DISTRICT OF COLUMBIA

DORAN INTERNATIONAL
P.O. Box 25762 Georgetown
Washington, DC 20007
Phone: 202-333-6367
Fax: 202-296-2391
Email: doranmodels@hotmail.com

KIMBERLY SKYRME AND JOHN COHN
SKYRME PICTURES INTERNATIONAL
1718 M Street, NW
Unit 298
Washington, DC 20036

FLORIDA

ALEXA MODEL & TALENT
4100 W Kennedy Blvd., Suite 228,

Tampa, Fl 33609
(813) 289-8020

ALLIANCE TALENT GROUP
10200 State Rd 84, Suite 300
Tampa, Fl 33325
(954) 727-9500

ARTHUR ARTHUR (Miami) INC.   (Tampa Area Office)
South Hillsborough Office Comp,
6542 US Hwy. 41 North
Apollo Beach, Fl 33572
(813) 645-9700

ARTHUR ARTHUR (Miami) INC.
245 S.E First St., Suite 406
Miami, FL 33131
(305)995-5889

AUGIE LASSETER
Front Management
311 Lincoln Road
Suite 310
Miami Beach, FL 33139
Phone: 305-673-2225
Fax: 786-276-8880
Cell: 305-632-6919
Web: www.frontmanagement.com

AZUREE TALENT INC.   (Orlando Area Office)
1115 Kentucky Ave.
Winter Park, FL 32789

(407) 629-5025

BACKGROUND ENTERTAINMENT EXTRAS CASTING
COMPANY
4390 35th Street
Orlando, Fl 3280
(407) 516-1855
www.backgroundentertainment.com

BELL, SANDI TALENT AGENCY   (Orlando Area Agency)
2582 S. Maguire Road, Suite 171
Ocoee Fl, 34761
(407) 445-9221

BENZ MODEL-TALENT AGENCY
1313 E. 8th Ave., 3rd Floor
Tampa Fl, 33605-3611
(813) 242-4400
www.benzmodels.com

BERG TALENT & MODEL AGENCY
15908 Eagle River Way
Tampa, FL 33624
(813)877-5533

BICOASTAL TALENT, INC.
398 West Amelia Street
Orlando, Fl 32801
(407) 839-4400

BOCA TALENT AND MODEL AGENCY   (Ft. Lauderdale Area Agency)
829 SE 9th Street

Deerfield Beach, Fl 33441
(954) 428-4400

BOCA TALENT & MODEL AGENCY
851 N. Market Street
Jacksonville, FL 32202
(904)356-4244

BREVARD TALENT GROUP, INC.
301 East Pine Street
Orlando, Fl 32801
(407) 841-7775
Fax (407) 841-7716
www.brevardtalentgroup.com

BURTON & ROBINSON AGENCY   (Port Charlotte
Area Agency)
361 W. Marion Ave.
Punta Gorda, FL 33950
(941) 575-9716

CENTRAL FLORIDA TALENT
5400 International Dr
Orlando Fl, 32819
(407) 370-2790
Fax (407) 370-2793
www.cftalent.com

CHRISTENSEN GROUP   (Orlando
Area Agency)
4395 St. Johns Parkway
Sanford, Fl 32771
(407) 302-2272

COCONUT GROVE TALENT AGENCY
(Miami Area Agency)
3525 Vista Court
Coconut Grove, Fl 33133
(305) 858-3002

CYNTHIA MODEL & TALENT AGENCY
7777 131st Street North, Suite 11
Seminole, Fl 33776
(727) 395-0674

DIAMOND AGENCY, INC. The   (Orlando Area
Agency)
585 East State Road 434, Suite #201
Longwood, Fl 32750
(407) 830-4040

DOTT BURNS MODEL & TALENT
478 Severn Ave., Davis Island
Tampa, FL 33606
(813)251-5882

EMERGE TALENT LLC
1013 E. Colonial Drive
Orlando, FL 32803
(321)293-0294

1111 Lincoln Road
Suite 400
Miami Beach, FL 33139
(305)434-7019

Holly Caputo

NY PH: (646)355-4592
TA#818info@emergetalent.com
www.emergetalent.com

FAMOUS FACES ENT Co
3780 SW 30th Avenue
Fort Lauderdale, Fl 33312
(954) 321-8883

GREEN AGENCY, INC.
1329 Alton Road
Miami Beach, Fl 33139
(305) 532-9225

HURT AGENCY TALENT AND MODELS   (Orlando
Area Agency)
400 N New York Ave. Suite #207
Winter Park, Fl 32789
(407) 740-5700

IN ANY EVENT
140 S. Atlantic Ave. 5th Floor
Ormond Beach, Fl 32176
(386) 676-2223

INTERNATIONAL ARTIST GROUP, INC.
2121 North Bayshore Dr. Suite 2E
Miami, Fl 33137
(305) 576-0001

LOUISE'S PEOPLE MODEL & TALENT AGENCY

863 13th Avenue North
St. Petersburg, Fl 33701
(7270 823-7828

MARIE, IRENE AGENCY
728 Ocean Drive
Miami Beach, Fl 33139
(305) 672-2929

MARTIN & DONALD'S TALENT AGENCY, INC.
2131 Hollywood Bvld. #308
Hollywood, Fl 33020
(954) 921-2427

McMILLIAN TALENT AGENCY, ROXANNE
12100 NE 16th Ave. Suite #106
Miami, Fl 33161
(305) 899-9150

POLAN TALENT AGENCY, MARION
10 NE 11th Ave.
Fort Lauderdale, Fl 33301
(954)525-8351

RUNAWAYS, THE TALENT GROUP
1688 Meridian Ave. Suite 500
Miami Beach, Fl 33139
(305)673-8245

SHEFFIELD AGENCY, INC.
800 West Avenue, Suite C-1
Miami Beach, FL 33139
(305)531-5886

STELLER TALENT AGENCY
927 Lincoln Road, Suite 2K
Miami Beach, Fl 33139
(305) 672-2217

STEWART'S MODELING. EVELYN
911 Samy Drive
Tampa, Fl 33613
(813) 968-1441

STRICKLY SPEAKING, INC.
711 Executive Dr.
Winter Park, FL 32789
(407) 645-2111

WILHELMINA-MIAMI
927 Lincoln Road, Suite 200
Miami Beach, Fl 33139
(305) 672-9344

WORLD OF KIDS INC.
1460 Ocean Drive, Suite 205
Miami Beach, Fl 33139
(305) 672-5437

GEORGIA

ATLANTA MODELS & TALENT, INC.
2970 Peachtree Road, NW, Suite #660
Atlanta, GA 30305
(404)261-9627

TED BORDEN & ASSOCIATES
2434 Adina Drive, NE, Suite B
Atlanta, GA 30324
(404)266-0664

THE BURNS AGENCY
602 Hammett Drive
Decatur, GA 30032
Tel: 404-299-8114
Fax: 404-299-8051
E-mail: burnSCREEN ACTORS
GUILDy@mindspring.com
SCREEN ACTORS GUILD/AFTRA

ELITE MODEL MANAGEMENT CORP/ATLANTA
181 14th Street, Suite #325
Atlanta, GA 30309
(404)872-7444

GLYN KENNEDY MODELS & TALENT
975 Hunter Hill Dr.,
Roswell, GA 30075
(678)461-4444

THE PEOPLE STORE
2004 Rockledge Road NE, Suite 60
Atlanta, GA 30324
(404)874-6448

THE TALENT GROUP/HOT SHOT KIDS
3300 Buckeye Road, Suite 405, Buckeye Tower
Atlanta, GA 30341
(770)986-9600

ELITE IMAGE PROMOTIONS/JOKERS WILD TALENT
Cherie Boston
12 East Main Street
Hampton, GA 30228
678-432-6840
678-463-5169

TIME AND PLACE TALENT GROUP
P.O. Box 387
Athens, GA 30601-2758
(706) 983-9760

IDAHO
CRAZE AGENCY
410 S. Orchard St. Suite 164
Boise, Idaho 83705
Phone: 208-433-9511
Web: www.crazeagency.com
e-mail crazeagency@sisna.com
Member BBB
Contact: Troy Lee

INDIANA

ARTISTIC ENTERPRISE, INC.
5350 E. 62nd Street
Indianapolis, IN 46235
(317) 722-1717
FAZ: (317) 722-1718
e-mail: seymore@iquest.net
Web: www.artisticindy.com

ILLINOIS

AMBASSADOR TALENT AGENTS
333 N. Michigan Ave, Suite 314
Chicago, IL 60601
(312) 641-3491

ARIA MODEL & TALENT MGMT.
1017 W. Washington Street, #2A
Chicago, IL 60607
(312) 243-9400

ARLENE WILSON TALENT, INC.
430 W. Erie Street, Suite 210
Chicago, IL 60610
(312) 573-0200

NAKED VOICES
865 N. Sangamon, Suite 415
Chicago, IL 60622
(312) 563-0136
FAX: (312) 563-0137

CUNNINGHAM ESCOTT DIPENE
(312) 944-5600

DAVID & LEE
641 W Lake Street, Suite 402
Chicago, IL 60661
(312) 670-4444

ENCORE TALENT AGENCY
1732 W. Hubbard Street

Chicago, IL 60622
(312) 738-0230
Fax: (312) 738- 0233

ETA INC.
7558 S. Chicago Ave
Chicago, IL 60619
(773) 753-3955

LINDA JACK TALENT
230 East Ohio Street, Suite 200
Chicago, IL 60611
(312) 587-1155

JEFFERSON & ASSOCIATES
1050 N. State Street
Chicago, IL 60610
(312) 337-1930

LILY'S TALENT AGENCY
1301 W. Washington Blvd.
Chicago, IL 60607
(312) 601-2345
Fax: (312) 601-2353
Web: www.liliystalent.com

MODEL & TALENT MANAGEMENT
3340 Dundee Rd
Northbrook, IL 60062
(847) 509-8583
Fax: (847) 509-8619
Web: www.mtmmodel.com

E-mail: agency@mtmmodel.com

SALAZR & NAVAS, INC.
760 N. Ogden Ave, Suite 2200
Chicago, IL 60622
(312) 751-3419

NORMAN SCHUCART ENTERTAINMENT
1417 Green Bay Rd
Highland Park, IL 60035
(847) 433-1113

STEWART TALENT MANAGEMENT
58 West Huron
Chicago, IL 60610
(312) 943-3131

VOICES UNLIMITED, INC
541 N. Fairbanks Ct, #28
Chicago, IL 60611
(312) 642-3262

LOUISIANA

PROFESSIONAL MODEL & TALENT SERVICES
P.O. Box 24428
New Orleans, LA 70124-4428
Fax: 504-828-9618

MARYLAND

CENTRAL CASTING (Baltimore) same policy as the Washington, D.C. office

2229 N. Charles Street
Baltimore, Maryland 21218

THE CASTING COMPANY
7315 Wisconsin Avenue Suite 705 east
Bethesda MD 20814 - 1155
Phone: 301-951-2010
Fax: 301-951-4428
Web: www.capcasting.com

SPICER PRODUCTIONS
1708 Whitehead Road
Baltimore, Maryland 21207

INDIGO PRODUCTIONS
4313 Hamilton Street
Hyattsville, Maryland 20781

ACCURATE CASTING & TALENT
1889 Grempler Way
Edgewood, Maryland 21040

STEELE CASTING
P.O. Box 969
Glen Burnie, Maryland 21060

KIDS INTERNATIONAL TALENT AGENCY
938 East Swan Creek Rd., Suite 152
Ft. Washington, MD 20744
301-292-6094

THE BULLOCK AGENCY
5200 Baltimore Avenue, Suite 102

Hyattsville, MD 20781
(301)209-9598

PAT MORAN & ASSOCIATES
c/o The Broom Factory
1301 Baylif, Suite 425
Baltimore, Maryland 21224

CAPITAL CASTING
7315 Wisconsin Avenue
Suite 705 East
Bethesda, MD 20814
Phone: 301-951-2010
Fax: 301-951-4428
Web: www.capcasting.com
E-mail: capcasting@aol.com

TAYLOR ROYALL CASTING
6247 Falls Rd
Baltimore, MD 21209
Phone: 410-828-1280
Fax: 410-828-1281

MASSACHUSETTS

THE MODELS GROUP
374 Congress Street, Suite #305
Boston, MA 02210
(617)426-4711

MODEL CLUB, INC.
115 Newbury St., Ste 203
Boston, MA 02116

(617)247-9020

MODELS, INC,
218 Newbury Street
Boston, MA 02116
(617)437-6212

MAGGIE, INC.
35 Newbury Street
Boston, MA 02116
(617)536-2639

PRESTIGE MODEL AND TALENT AGENCY
7 Hampshire Street
Methuen, MA 01844
Phone: 978-687-3333
E-mail prestige28@juno.com

MICHIGAN

AFFILIATED MODELS, INC.
1680 Crooks Road
Troy, MI 48084
Phone: 248-244-8770
Fax: 248-244-8731
Website: www.AffiliatedGroup.com

MINNESOTA

CARYN MODEL & TALENT
Butler Square Bldg.
100 N. 6th St., #270B
Minneapolis, MN 55403

(612) 349-3600

MEREDITH MODELS & Talent
800 Washington Avenue North
Suite 511
Minneapolis, MN 55401
(612) 340-9555

MOORE CREATIVE CASTING, INC.
1610-B West Lake Street
Minneapolis, MN 55408
(612) 827-3823

NEW FACES MODELS & TALENT INC.
6301 Wayzata Blvd.
Minneapolis, MN 55416
(612) 544-8668

THE WEHMANN AGENCY
1128 Harmon Place, #205
Minneapolis, MN 55403
(612) 333-6393

JMG Model and Talent
PO Box 251201
St. Paul, MN 55125
651-734-9618 - office
651-734-9642 - fax
E-mail: jwenzel3@hotmail.com

MISSOURI

MILLENNIUM MODEL AND TALENT MANAGEMENT

511 Delaware
Loft 100
Kansas City, MO 64105
Contact: Reina Sonda
E-mail: tgroman@millennium-models.com
www.millennium-models.com
816-474-8383

NEW YORK

ABRAMS ARTIST AGENCY LTD
275 Seventh Avenue, 26th Floor
New York, NY 10001
Phone: (646) 486-4600

ACME TALENT & LITERARY AGENCY
60 Madison Ave, 2nd Floor
New York, NY 10010
Phone: (212)328-0387

AGENCY FOR PERFORMING ARTS
888 Seventh Avenue, 6th Floor
New York, NY 10106
Phone: (212) 582-1500

AGENTS FOR THE ARTS INC.
203 West 23rd Street, 3rd Floor
New York, NY 10011
Phone: (212) 229-2562

ALLIANCE TALENT INCORPORATED
1501 Broadway, Suite 404
New York, NY 10036

Phone: (212) 840-6868

MICHAEL AMATO THEATRICAL ENTERPRISE
1650 Broadway, Suite 307
New York, NY 10019
Phone: (212) 247-4456

AMERICAN INTERNATIONAL TALENT
303 West 42nd Street, Suite 608
New York, NY 10036
Phone: (212) 245-8888

BARRY HAFT BROWN ARTIST
165 West 46th Street, Suite 908
New York, NY 10036
Phone: (212) 229-2562

BETHEL AGENCY
P.O. Box 21043
Park West Station
New York, NY 10025
(212) 864-4510

311 West 43rd Street, Suite 602
New York, NY 10036
(212) 664-0455

BIG DUKE SIX ARTIST AGENCY
220 Fifth Ave, Suite 800
New York, NY 10001
(212) 989-6927

CARRY COMPANY

49 West 46th Street, 4th Floor
New York, NY 10036
(212) 768-2793

THE CARSON ORGANIZATION, LTD
240 West 44th Street, Penthouse 12
(212) 221-1517

CLASSIC MODEL & TALENT MANAGEMENT, INC
87 South Finley Avenue
Basking Ridge, NY 07920
(908) 766-6663

HENDERSON/HOGAN AGENCY INC.
850 Seventh Avenue, Suite 1003
New York, NY 10019
(212) 765-5190

INTERNATIONAL CREATIVE MANAGEMENT
40 West 57th Street
New York, NY 10019
(212) 556-5600

JAM THEATRICAL AGENCY, INC.
352 Seventh Avenue, Suite 1500
New York, NY 10001
(212) 376-6330

BERNARD LIEHABER AGENCY
352 Seventh Avenue
New York, NY 10001
(212) 631-7561

NOUVELLE TALENT MANAGEMENT, INC.
20 Bethune Street, Suite 3B
New York, NY 10014
(212) 645-0940

DOROTHY PALMER TALENT AGENCY
235 West 56th Street, #24K
New York NY 10019
(212) 765-4280

PROFESSIONAL ARTIST UNLTD
321 West 44th Street, #24K
New York NY 10036
(212) 247-8770

PYRAMID ENTERTAINMENT GROUP
89 Fifth Avenue
New York, NY 10003

SAMES & ROLLNICK ASSOCIATES
250 West 57th Street, Suite 703
New York, NY 10107
(212) 315-4434

KIMBERLY SKYRME
SKYRME LEWIS AND FOX CASTING
459 Columbus Avenue
Unit 164
New York, NY 10024

SPECIAL ARTIST AGENCY, INC.
220 Fifth Ave, 19th Floor Penthouse West

New York, NY 10001
(212) 420-0200

STANLEY KAPLAN TALENT
139 Fulton Street, Suite 503
New York, NY 10038
(212) 385-4400

ANN STEELE AGENCY
330 W 42nd Street
New York, NY 10036
(212) 629-9112

HANNS WOLTERS INTERNATIONAL INC.
211 E 43rd Street, #505
New York, NY 10017
(212) 714-0100

ANN WRIGHT REPRESENTATIVE, INC.
165 West 46th Street
New York, NY 10036
(212) 764-6770

WRITERS & ARTIST AGENCY
19 West 44th Street, Suite 1000
New York, NY 10036
(212) 391-1112

NORTH CAROLINA

TALENT LINK INC.
P.O. Box 77185
Charlotte, NC 28271

Phone: 704-335-0027
Fax: 704-335-0027

OHIO

JO GOENNER TALENT AGENCY
4700 Reed Rd. Suite E
Columbus, Ohio 43220
(614)459-3582

CAM TALENT-CINCINATTI
1150 W. Eight St., #262
Cincinnati, OH 45203
(513) 421-1795

CAM TALENT - COLUMBUS
1350 West 5th Ave., Suite 25
Columbus, OH 43212
(614) 488-1122

CREATIVE TALENT
5864 Nike Drive
Hilliard, Ohio 43026
(614) 294-7827

HEYMAN TALENT, INC
3308 Brotherton
Cincinnati, OH 45209
(513) 533-3113

JO GOENNER TALENT AGENCY
10019 Paragon Rd.

Dayton, OH 45458
(937) 885--2595

SOURCE MODEL MANAGEMENT
8286 Kesegs Way
Blacklick, Ohio 43004
614-855-3179
kwrob@earthlink.net

GO-INTERNATIONAL MODEL MGMT. INC.
3351 Valley View Rd. NE
Lancaster, Ohio 43130 USA
Owner: Mona Grace Overton
614.554.6974
URL: http://go-international.com
Email: mona@go-international.com

IMI TALENT MANAGEMENT
9700 Rockside Rd Ste 410
Cleveland, Ohio 44125
Work: 216-901-9710
Fax: 216-901-9714
E-mail: Info@imitalent.com
Web: www.imitalent.com

MODEL & TALENT MANAGEMENT
256 Easton Town Center
Columbus, OH. 43219
Phone: (614) 472-2207
Fax: (614) 472-2205
Web: www.mtmmodel.com
Email: agency@mtmmodel.com

PENNSYLVANIA

THE CLARO MODELING AGENCY
1513 West Passyunk Ave
Philadelphia, PA 19145
(215)465-7788

EXPRESSIONS MODELING & TALENT
110 Church Street
Philadelphia, PA 19106
(215)923-4420

JAGUAR PRODUCTIONS, INC. (film, video & management co.)
35 Golf Rd.
Upper Darby, PA 19082
Phone: (610) 352-3585
Fax: (215) 731-0635
E-mail - dpowe38024@aol.com
Contact: Delayne Powe (business coordinator)

THE REINHARD AGENCY
2021 Arch Street, Suite 400
Philadelphia, PA 19103
(215)567-2008

THE T.G. AGENCY
2820 Smallman Street
Pittsburgh, PA 15222
(412)471-8011

THE TALENT GROUP
2820 Smallman Street

Pittsburgh, PA 15222
(412) 471-8011

MIKE LEMON CASTING
413 North 7th Suite 602
Philadelphia, PA 19123
TONI CUSUMANO CASTING
PO Box 839
Stroudsburg PA 18360
Phone: 212-712-784
Web: www.tonicusumano.com

SOUTH CAROLINA

MAXANN'S CASTING COMPANY
Maxann Crotts
PO Box 4137
745-122 Saluda Street
Rock Hill, SC 29732-6137
803-328-3420(o)
803-324-8700(fax)
email: maxann@maxannscastingcompany.com
website: www.maxannscastingcompany.com

TENNESSEE

DS ENTERTAINMENT
AGENT: DARLENE STUDIE-McDOWELL
9005 OVERLOOK BOULEVARD
BRENTWOOD, TN 37027
Phone: 615-331-6264
Fax: 615-837-8227
website: www.dsentertainment.com

email address: darlene@dsentertainment.com
SPECIALTY: We promote talent/models for commercials, videos, film, television, industrials, print, promotional modeling & runway.

TEXAS

ACCLAIM TALENT
4100 Manchaca Road
Austin, Texas 78704
Phone: 512-416-9222
Fax: 512-416-9111
www.acclaimtalent.com

ACTORS, ETC
2620 Fountainview, Suite #210
Houston, TX 77057
(713)785-4495

ASPA (Asian Star Productions & Agency, Inc.)
11311 Harry Hines Blvd. # 503
Dallas, TX 75229
Tel: (972) 481-9661
Fax: (972) 484-5504
E-mail: aspa2000_us@yahoo.com
Web: http://www.asianstarproduction.com

THE CAMPBELL AGENCY
3906 Lemmon Avenue, Suite 200
Dallas, TX 75219
(214)522-8991

CONDRA ARTIST TALENT AGENCY

Booking Agents: Mary Vara and Heidi Kyle
10737 Gulfdale Ste 200 San Antonio, TX 78216
Website: www.condraartista.com
Tel: 210.492.9947
Fax: 210.492.9921

KIM DAWSON AGENCY
700, Tower North, 2710 N.
Stemmons Freeway
Dallas, TX 75207
(214)630-5161

DOUBLE TAKE TALENT AGENCY
14902 Preston Road, Suite 404-324
Dallas, TX 75240
(972)404-4436

NEAL HAMIL AGENCY
7887 San Felipe, Suite 204,
Houston, TX 77063
(713)789-1335

INTERMEDIA TALENT AGENCY
2727 Kirby, Penthouse
Houston, TX 77098
(713)622-8282

MARQUEE TALENT, INC.
5911 Maple Avenue,
Dallas, TX 75235
(214)357-0355

SHERRY YOUNG AGENCY

2620 Fountain View, Suite #212
Houston, TX 77057
(713)266-5800

PEGGY TAYLOR TALENT
437 Southfork
Suite 400
Lewisville, TX 75067
Phone: 214-651-7884
Fax: f214-651-7FAX
Web: www.peggytaylortalent.com
E-mail: peggy@peggytaylortalent.com

TOMAS AGENCY
14275 Midway Road, Suite 200
Addison, TX 75001
(972)687-9181

WILLIAMS TALENT, INC.
13313 SW Freeway, Suite 194
Sugar Land, TX 77478
Phone: 281-240-1080
Fax: 281-240-1077

CIAO! TALENTS
1310 E. University
Georgetown, Texas 78626
Phone: (512) 930-9301
Fax: (512) 930-9302
Web: www.CiaoTalents.com
Email: CiaoTalents@bigfoot.com

DIANE DICK INTERNATIONAL MODELING AND TAL-
ENT AGENCY
1410 S. Washington
Amarillo, Texas. 79102
Phone: 806-376-8736
Fax: 806-376-8841
Email: Ddleg@aol.com

UTAH

CRAZE AGENCY
9192 S. 300 W. #2
Sandy, UT 84070
Phone: 801-438-0067
Web: www.crazeagency.com
e-mail crazeagency@sisna.com
Member BBB
Contact: Troy Lee

KNIGHTSTAR MULTIMEDIA, LLC
P.O. Box 893
Lehi, UT 84043
Office: (801) 789-2665
Fax: (801) 789-8231
E-mail: KnightTalent@gmail.com
Website: www.KnightStarTalent.com

VIRGINIA

CARLYN DAVIS CASTING
207 Park Avenue, Suite B6
Falls Church, VA 22046

THE AMBASSADOR TALENT AGENCY
P.O. Box 1027, Stanardsville, Virginia 22973
Phone: (804) 978-1742
E-Mail: todd_sherrod@hotmail.com
Contact Name: Todd Sherrod, Yelitza Sherrod
Small independent agency which represents all types (Union &
Non-Union) for film, television, industrials, and independent
features. Special interest in Christian film projects. Seek talent
primarily in Washington D.C. and New York City/New Eng-
land regions. Accepts photos and resumes. Please no phone
calls.

TALENT LINK
325 E. Bayview Blvd.
Suite 203
Norfolk, VA 23503

All headshot submissions should be sent to:
Talent Link
P.O. Box 12007
Newport News, VA 23612

WASHINGTON

ACTORS GROUP
114 Alaskan Way South, Suite 104
Seattle, WA 98104
(206)624-9465

DRAMATIC ARTISTS AGENCY
1000 Lenora Street, Suite 501
Seattle, WA 98121
(206)442-9190

ENTCO INTERNATIONAL, Inc.
7017 196TH ST SW
Lynnwood, WA 98036
(425) 670-0888

HEFFNER MANAGEMENT
Westlake Center
1601 Fifth Ave., Suite 2301
Seattle, WA 98101
(206) 622-2211

KID BIZ TALENT AGENCY
One Bellevue Center
411 108th Ave., N.E., Suite 2050
Bellevue, WA 98004
(206) 455-8800

SEATTLE MODELS GUILD
1809 Seventh Ave., Suite 303
Seattle, WA 98101
(206) 622-1406

TOPO SWOPE TALENT AGENCY
1932 1st Ave., Suite 700
Seattle, WA 98101
(206) 443-2021

CANADA
Canadian talent should also check out the ACTRA (Alliance of Canadian Cinema, Television and Radio Artists) web site at:
www.actra.com

ANGIE'S TALENT
25A York Street
Ottawa, Ontario K1N 5S7 Canada
Tel: 613-244-0544 (Ottawa)
http://www.angiesmodels.com/

ANGIE'S MODEL & IMAGES
25 A York Street & 4 Second St. East
Ottawa, Ontario K1N 5S7 or Cornwall Ontario K6H 1Y3
CANADA
Tel: 613-932-1451 (Cornwall)
Tel: 613-244-0544 (Ottawa)
http://www.angiesmodels.com/

ELITE CASTING
3981 St. Laurent Blvd.
Suite 700
Montreal, Quebec, Canada H2W 1Y5
Phone: 514-282-1631
Fax: 514-844-8223

DEB GREEN CASTING
Box 232, 16 Midlake Blvd. SE
Calgary, Alberta, Canada T2X 2X7
Phone: 403-931-3181

NOVA TALENT
179 Strachan Ave.
Toronto, On. Canada M6J 2T1
Phone 416-504-1837
Email: emc2@connection.com
Edward McLaughlin, Agent

THE PLAYERS GROUP
620A Bloor Street West, Suite 301
Toronto, Ont. M6G 1K7
Phone: 416-536-4505
Fax: 416-536-2145

STEEL TOWN TALENT
Hamilton, Ontario
in Canada toll free at 1-800-530-5842
outside Canada (905) 312-8439
Fax (905) 312-0356
steeltowntalent@on.aibn.com
Scott R.J Lester

UNIONS

ARIZONA

SCREEN ACTORS GUILD
3131 E. Camelback Road, Suite 200
Phoenix, Arizona 85016
(602) 383-3780
(800) 724-0767 (Toll Free)
Fax: (602) 383-3781
The Arizona Office also covers Utah.

CALIFORNIA

SCREEN ACTORS GUILD
5757 Wilshire Blvd
Los Angeles, CA 90036-3600
(323) 954-1600

Fax: (323) 549-6603
For Deaf Performers Only – TTY/TTD (323) 549-6648
This office covers Nevada, as well as San Diego c/o Hrair
Messerlian.

SCREEN ACTORS GUILD
350 Sansome Street, Suite 900
San Francisco, CA 94104
(415) 391-7510
Fax: 391-1108

COLORADO

SCREEN ACTORS GUILD
Market Square Center
1400 Sixteenth Street Suite 400
Denver, CO 80202
(720) 932-8193
Fax: (720) 932-8194
Fax Toll Free: (800) 595-4256
This office covers New Mexico c/o Julie Crane.

FLORIDA

SCREEN ACTORS GUILD
(Central Florida, Orlando Area)
522 Hunt Club Blvd. #410
Apopka, Florida 32703
(407) 788-3020
Fax: (407) 788-3080

(Miami) South Region Office
7300 North Kendall Drive, Suite #620

Miami, Florida 33156-7840
(305) 670-7677
Fax local (305) 670-1813
Fax Toll Free (800) 844-5439
This office also covers Tennessee c/o Leslie Krensky, as well
as North Carolina c/o Melodie Shaw

GEORGIA

SCREEN ACTORS GUILD
455 E. Paces Ferry Road NE, Suite 334
Atlanta, GA 30305
(404) 239-0131
Fax: (404) 239-0137

HAWAII

SCREEN ACTORS GUILD
949 Kapiolani Blvd, #105
Honolulu, HI 96814
(808) 262-8001
Fax: (808) 596-0388
Fax Toll Free: (808) 593-2636

ILLINOIS

SCREEN ACTORS GUILD
1 East Erie, Suite 650
Chicago, IL 60611
(312) 573-8081
Fax: (312) 573-0318
Fax: (800) 599-1675

The Chicago Office also Cleveland, Minneapolis, and St. Louis)

MARYLAND
(Washington DC/ Baltimore)

SCREEN ACTORS GUILD
4340 East West Highway-Suite 204
Bethesda, Maryland 20814
(301) 657-2560
Fax: (301) 656-3615
Fax Toll Free: (800) 253-9730

MASSACHUSETTS

SCREEN ACTORS GUILD
535 Boylston Street
Boston, MA 02116
(617) 262-8001
Fax: (617) 262-3006
Fax: (800) 737-6105 (Toll Free)

MICHIGAN

SCREEN ACTORS GUILD
Town Center
2000 Town Center Suite 1900
Southfield, MI 48075
(248) 351-2678
Fax: (248) 351-2679

NEW YORK

SCREEN ACTORS GUILD
360 Madison Avenue
New York, NY 10017
(212) 944-1030
Fax: (212) 944-6774
For Deaf Performers Only – TTY/TTD (212) 944-6715
This office covers Philadelphia c/o Jae Je Simmons

TEXAS

SCREEN ACTORS GUILD
15950 N. Dallas Parkway
Dallas, TX 75248
(972) 361-8185
Fax: (972) 361-8186
(800) 311-3216 (Toll Free)
This office covers Houston c/o Henry Kana, and works in conjunction with south regional office in Miami Florida.

WASHINGTON

SCREEN ACTORS GUILD
4000 Aurora Ave N #102
Seattle, WA 98103
(206) 270-0493
Fax: (206) 270-7073

This office covers Oregon c/o Dena Beatty toll free (800) 724-0767.

Glossary of Terms

Audition: a process to cast actors and actresses in a production, also know as try outs.

Casting Director: one who decides which actor is to appear in a production.

Composite: 5 ½ X 8 ½ cards consisting of three photos and stats used for modeling.

Director: one in charge of production, stage or screen.

Extra: an actor without a speaking role, whose sole purpose is to appear in the background.

Extra Casting Company: a company whose sole existence is to provide extras, many talent agencies start out this way.

Featured Extra: and extra mentioned in the credits

First Unit: the production crew and principal actors

Headshot: an 8X10 professional photograph used for the purpose of casting; generally colored prints for screen, and black and white for stage.

On Location: the actual location where the story takes place, not a sound stage, out door location.

Perpetuity: to own someone's image and reuse it for infinity without compensation.

Principal Actor: the actors that are cast with speaking roles.

Producer: one who supervises and finance the making of a television, or film production.

Production: a presentation of television, film, or stage.

Rate of pay: the amount of money paid by the hour or day.

Residuals: money paid to principal actors every time a commercial airs.

Resume: a summary of ones acting experience.

Second Unit: usually the stunt crew and stunt actors

Set: a place where the production is filmed.

Stand In: a person who stands in place for a principal actor while the shot is being set up or established

Stats: information consisting of name, height, weight, hair color, eye color, clothing size and date of birth if under eighteen.

Sound Stage: a place of production within a studio.

Talent Agent: a person responsible for getting an actor or actress his or her job.

About the Author

My name is Daniel Whitehurst.

Ever since I was three I knew I wanted to be an entertainer. I started my acting career in a drama class in my senior year at Walker High School in Atlanta. I made my first Debut in the Spring of 85 in the role of Assagi in a production called *Raisin in the Sun*. My teacher advised that I go to college and major in theatre, but I couldn't afford college, so I joined the Navy instead.

Five years later I moved to Orlando, and in January of 2000 I signed with Central Florida Talent and later with Azuree Talent who gave me my first shot to work as a regular extra in the television series *Sheena* and an episode of *Nickelodeon's Taina*.

I later trained under Shauna Bartel, and since then have worked in several commercials and one feature film. I currently work and live in Orlando Florida.

Made in the USA
Middletown, DE
12 January 2016